This book is dedicated to all those who have lived in Co

Giuliano (Julian) Carosi

The cover shows the BBC 1 Poldark series being filmed in the High Street in May 2014. The back cover is the same view along the High Street from the Town Hall.

At his leaving presentation when Police Inspector C.W. Perry resigned his Corsham post in September 1949, he told his friends the following........

"He came to Corsham sixteen and a half years ago as a Sergeant and among other things it fell to his duty to keep an eye on Corsham Court. He had learned to love that lovely old house in its beautiful setting, as he had learned to love Corsham, even more than the great Metropolis where he was born. He had tried to do his job without fear or favour, and he thanked them all for their great kindness to him."

[Ed] We love Corsham.

ISBN 978-1-5272-7770-0

Corsham Revealed Now and Then

This first edition was published by the author in November 2020

Printed by
Corsham Print Ltd.
Unit 4, Leafield Way,
Leafield Industrial Estate,
Corsham,
Wiltshire
SN13 9SW

ISBN 978-1-5272-7770-0

Please do not venture on private land without the owner's or proper permission.

More books by Giuliano (Julian) Carosi

The trilogy of 'Corsham Revealed' books.

This book contains a total of 240 Images

Julian Carosi

November 2020

Giuliano (Julian) Carosi.

Preface: Following the success and the interest shown in my trilogy of 'Corsham Revealed' books, 'Corsham Revealed' published in 2018, 'Corsham Revealed More' published in 2019, and 'Corsham Revealed Three' published in early 2020, I have produced this fourth book about our lovely town of Corsham, Wiltshire. There is so much to know about this little sleepy town, that every time I turn over the leaf of an old book or newspaper, or happen to come across an ancient Corsham story in the bottomless pit of the *Internet* - I want to share it with others. When a new door opens into Corsham's past, it often leads me into other rooms with multiple-doors that revealed *more* facts that have long been lost. In fact, there is still so much more out there to find…………………all it needs is time and enthusiasm to collate it all.

In my first book *'Corsham Revealed'*, I mentioned how the idea about writing a book on Corsham's history came to me over forty years ago, when I surprisingly *beat* my Regis Primary School teacher Mr Williams in a *'Know Your Corsham'* history competition. The prize then, was a small amount of cash. The even bigger prize now - is the joy I see on peoples' faces when they greet me in Corsham High Street with, *"Are you Julian?"* or when they give me even more Corsham facts to digest.

As a child growing up in Corsham, there were no technical contraptions to keep children indoors. We created our own adventures by delving into every corner (above and below ground) of Corsham that we could - and even some corners that we shouldn't have!

In this, my fourth book titled *'Corsham Revealed Now and Then'*, my aim is to share with you even *more* of what I have found. You don't necessarily have to read this book from cover to cover; you can dip your toe in from time to time into any page that catches your fancy. Inside, you will find even *more* hidden, long-forgotten and sometimes mysterious historical snippets of Corsham. In this book you'll find 100 different aspects of Corsham compared over many years. The emphasis is more on providing pairs of photographs accompanied with a small amount of respective text to show just how much Corsham has changed or conversely how little it has changed over the ensuing years. Further detailed information and additional photographs on some of the subjects included here, can be found in my 'Corsham Revealed' trilogy of books.

Gathering this information required many hours of research spent *head down* reading, tapping away on my computer and rummaging in the brilliant Wiltshire and Swindon History Centre in Chippenham, trawling through their newspaper archives; interrogation of the internet, purchasing historical books, postcards and maps, and even more hours walking around our beautiful town of Corsham. The last effort in putting this book together required a further six months of sifting through the huge amount of material collected and then piecing it all together - to rewrite and produce this, my fourth Corsham Revealed book *[Corsham Revealed Now and Then]* that I hope you will enjoy.

Now, please let me take you on another journey that will hopefully change your perception of Corsham; but I make no apologies for the remarkable and memorable findings. Enjoy.

Contents of 'Corsham Revealed Now and Then' in alphabetical order showing page numbers:

Corsham Revealed Now and Then - Introduction

Corsham is blessed with historians present and past. In **1924** Harold Brakspear, F.S.A. wrote a detailed book titled *'Corsham Church'* covering the history of St. Bartholomew's church. In **1979** Patricia Whalley captured the *'History of Royal Naval Store Depot Copenacre'* in a small pamphlet. In **2009** she managed to fill her small book *'Corsham Facts & Folklore'* with oh so many interesting snippets of Corsham history and followed this up in **2012** with *'Corsham Memories The Prefab Years'* and later with *'The Shadow Mary Dean'* story in **2015**. Nobody has done more than Patricia Whalley to get Corsham's history into print for future generations to enjoy. In **1981** Faith Sharp and Heather Tanner blessed us with *'A Corsham Boyhood'*, the diary of Herbert Spackman 1877-1891, a story of one of Corsham's most famous inhabitants whose photographic images created iconic memories of Corsham. In **1983** Bob Hayward wrote *'Memories of a Village boyhood in GASTARD, Wiltshire'*. In March **1983** Christopher J. Hall produced the first of his two books entitled *'An Illustrated History'*, and later *'Tanky Elms'* the Bath Stone quarryman, all fabulous mini-archives of Corsham that most inhabitants have already enjoyed browsing through. John Poulsom provided a detailed general history when he published his book *'The Ways of Corsham'* in **1989** with help from his daughter Vivienne and photographs from another local historian Joe James. The end product was 80 pages ranging from the origins of Corsham Parish to a potted history which included the surrounding villages. In **1989** Corsham Dr Peter Henderson's small booklet *'Twelve and a Half Footpath Walks in Corsham Parish'* was on the bookshelves. In **1995** he also produced a very detailed book marking the first *'100 Years in Corsham Parish'* and filled it with life as it was here between1894 to 1994. In **1990** Annette Wilson and Mike Wilson's *'Around Corsham and Box in old photographs'* book appeared. Then in **1991** came Stephen Flavin, who went on to produce two volumes of *'Corsham Born and Bred'*; these books that can probably be found resting on most Corsham house bookshelves! In **1997** Ernest Hird produced the grandly titled *'The Lady Margaret Hungerford Almshouse and Free School, Corsham, Wiltshire 1668-1968'* a book full to the rafters with meticulous detail covering one of Corsham's iconic buildings. In **2008** he produced *'A Life Revealed From the Diaries of Herbert Spackman'* a very detailed account of one of Corsham's most famous inhabitants. In **1997** the Corsham Civic Society produced *'The Archived Photographs series Corsham'* compiled by Anne Lock and reprinted it in **2011** renaming it *'Around Corsham'*. In **2004** and **2006** Dennis Williams wrote two books in memory of his wife, *'Gwendolin'* and *'Gwendolin II'* revealing the secrets of working in the underground city here in Corsham during WWII. In In **2011** the Civic Society also produced *'Corsham Memories from 1910'*. In **2018** Kevin Gaskin edited and produced *'Corsham Commemorates'* a beautiful booklet capturing the lives of the Corsham men who died or were killed in the Great War - a duty nobly done.

Apologies if I have missed out any other Corsham books that should have appeared in the above list. Most of the above were produced in the days before computers took over the world. I have great admiration for all the authors and editors mentioned above, for all their hard work in producing a splendid picture of our beautiful town of Corsham.

I'm very proud to add my four *'Corsham Revealed'* books to this ever growing list - and may it continue to be added to by others in future years. My fourth book *'Corsham Revealed Now and Then'* is a pictorial view of 100 aspects of Corsham that makes the town what it is today - such a lovely place to live in. Enjoy.

Julian Carosi

Almshouses: The 1668 Corsham Schoolroom and Almshouses were founded by Lady Margaret Hungerford. It was originally built to house six *poor people*. She lived with her husband Sir Edward Hungerford in nearby Corsham House (now Corsham Court). The enclosed stone walled yards in front of the *pentice* or cloister walkway at the rear of the houses, were for *'Poor people to hold Wood or Coal dust'*. The schoolmaster's house was in the outside angle of the building facing the road. Behind the large windows in the photos is the schoolroom which originally provided education for ten poor children. The building to the left *(out of picture)* was once a stable block (now apartments). Trustees continue to manage the property whilst volunteers guide visitors around the Master's house, schoolroom and exhibition room on open days.

Arnold House

High Street - Arnold House: Miss Pictor lived in Arnold House *(now the Corsham Heritage and Information Centre).* Although she hardly ever spent any money on herself, she kindly left her Arnold House property to Corsham Parish Council after she passed away in 1959...her ghost is said to walk the boards upstairs. She used to sit for hours at an upstairs window watching the inhabitants of Corsham going about their business below her. Opposite, in January 1849 Henry Spackman's grocery shop, was discovered to be on fire, and within a short time the whole of the premises, with its contents, was engulfed and Harold died after re-entering the premises. Below is Miss Mary Smith, the Corsham Congregational Church Festival May Queen, in procession with her Maids of Honour in 1938, accompanied by Corsham's *"county lads and lassies"*.

Bandstand

Bandstand: It was first used on Wednesday 14th July 1926 during the *'Children's Fourth Annual Sports Day'* at the Recreation Field. The Corsham Band had its first practice session there on the 11th July 1928. During WWII as a precaution against enemy bombing, the Parish Council considered using the bandstand as an air-raid shelter. Instead, a purpose built air-raid shelter was built at the bottom of the Recreation Field. After many years of neglect, the bandstand was in a poor shape and little used. It was finally demolished in 1958. No physical part of the bandstand remains above ground today. In 2018 unprecedented dry weather revealed a square imprint in the scorched grass of exactly where the bandstand was located at the top/centre in the field. The bandstand photo below was taken at a charity football match in 1956.

Corsham Bandstand 1956

Baptist Church

Baptist Church: The photo below shows the 26 October 1935 wedding at the Priory Street Baptist Church of Mr and Mrs Martin of Pickwick Road. Mr Martin was the Corsham Fire Chief. He was often seen in years gone by, frantically trying to gather the horses together (prior to the motorised vehicle) whenever the alarm was sounded. About 1822, some members of the Congregational Church in Corsham (now the Grounded Café), disagreed with their Church's doctrine and a new chapel was built in Priory Street. Uriah Blacker Goold was a co-founder of the Baptist Ebenezer Chapel, the stone to build it was provided free from Uriah's quarry in Velley Hill, Gastard. It opened on 1st January 1829. In 1838 a gallery was added and in 1867 the building was enlarged to include a vestry, the whole cost £300 (£24,000 in today's money).

Basil Hill Barracks

Queen Mary, wife of King George V

Basil Hill Barracks: The War Office bought the Basil Hill Barracks site in 1936. It was used in WWII by 15 Company Royal Army Ordnance Corps as the administrative headquarters for the underground Central Ammunitions Depot. Above is an aerial view of the barracks; below is Queen Mary's visit there in May 1941. Originally called the 21st Army Group Signals the 10th Signal Regiment was based here; they disbanded in 1987 and re-formed at Basil Hill in 2002 with 2 Signal Brigade. It was their job to protect troops in the field using the latest technology including cabling and telephones. The regiment can trace its origins back to Scotland in 1859. The Basil Hill site is now home to Defence Digital; in 2019 they combined and replaced a number of MoD organisations together, including Information Systems and Services (ISS).

Bath House

Corsham Court Bath House: This is a Grade I Gothic styled listed building. The sunken bath has steps leading into it and was designed c1761-3 by Lancelot Brown, altered 1797 and 1802 by J. Nash. The remnant of Brown's ground floor stonework was removed from the front arcade and incorporated in the Sham Ruin at the front of Corsham Court. The three arched portico entrance, beautifully frames the ancient sunken Roman bath (also known as The Cold Bath). The Cold Bath is sunk into an arcaded ground floor and a flight of steps leads up to a dressing room above. Nothing much has changed since the early 1900s on Tompkins & Barrett postcard below. The photo above shows the rear Bradford Porch, a summerhouse by E Tew incorporating late medieval stonework from The Priory in Bradford-on-Avon.

Batters

Batters: The Batters is a narrow managed woodland area that runs alongside the railway line and owned by Corsham Town Council. It has footpaths linking Prospect/Pound Pill with Brook Drive. The Ladbrook stream rises to the south and flows through modern housing eastwards through the Batters and out of the Parish to Lacock where it flows into the River Avon. The 'Batters' was put to good use in 1915/1916 for trench building exercises by the Scots Guards (see photo below) before they went off to war on the Western Front. Paul Sanford Methuen, 3rd Baron Methuen (1st September 1845 - 30th October 1932) the owner of Corsham Court was their Colonel-in-Chief. In November 2016 the Batters was protected with the erection of a centenary plaque as part of a national initiative by *Fields in Trust* and the *Royal British Legion*.

Beechfield

Beechfield: In 1946 Mr Clifford Ellis Headmaster of Bath School of Art was appointed as the Principal of the Corsham Court Training College and School of Art, named as the Bath Academy of Art (located at Corsham Court and Beechfield) which opened on 9 October of that year with at least 56 students. It was closed down in 1986. Bath Academy of Art then became Bath School of Art and Design which is now part of Bath University and has a presence once again in Corsham Court. The Beechfield Bath Art College Printing and Pottery House below (photo c1965) was converted to apartments in 2002 when Beechfield House was refurbished and the grounds landscaped into a beautiful park with luxury homes. In the 1940's the 'Beechfield' site was taken over by the military in WWII and the grounds were filled with timber huts.

Corsham Lake's Boathouse: The grade II listed Boathouse was built in the late C18th parkland by John Nash as a focal point *'eye-catcher'* at the far end of Corsham Lake. It survives today as a habitable 2-bed cottage, part of the Corsham Estate (the conversion was made many years ago). The picturesque gable end is occasionally visible across the lake from Corsham Court's Picture Gallery and for the enjoyment of walkers in Corsham Park, just as the lake builder Humphry Repton had intended - by displaying Nash's work to dramatic effect, framed by clumps of trees across undulating parkland as spectators pass along the original carriage drive. These days, the cottage often disappears behind the surrounding foliage. Below is a 1906 postcard image of the Boathouse. Above, it looks the same today ......at the far end of Corsham Lake.

Boltons: Number 79 High Street opposite the Flemish Buildings is known as Boltons. This is the oldest house now remaining in Corsham tithing. At the end of the reign of King Henry VIII it was owned by the family of Bolton, otherwise Tomson, who were in possession till 1597, when it was surrendered to Lawrence Kington, who in 1606 surrendered it to William Moxham, in whose family it remained till it passed through a daughter to John Wilshire. After John's death it went to widow Grace Hampton, a daughter of his sister, and in 1762 her son sold it to Paul Methuen. William Moxham left in his 1621 Will *"the sum of ten powndes"* for the poor *(nearly £3,000 in today's money);* the Newlands Road Moxhams flats are named after him. The two High Street houses alongside Boltons, were once a Temperance Hotel.

August 2019 complete turf renovation commences.

Bowls Club: The Corsham Bowls Club (one of the oldest in England) was founded in 1909 in Station Road at the bottom of the Cricket Field. The Herbert Spackman photo shown below, taken on 4 October 1918 on Corsham's Bowling green, shows a group of nurses and WWI wounded soldiers from the Voluntary Aid Detachment (VAD) Hospital in the Town Hall, enjoying a *'bowls'* day out (*see if you can spot the ghost!*) In 1924 the green was levelled with new turf to provide 4 rinks. In 1938 a woman's section was formed there. In 2019/2020 a new fence was installed to replace the hedge bordering the cricket field. The green was completely renovated including a new irrigation system and surrounding pathways completed, whilst the club was closed late 2019 and for the best part of 2020 due to the Coronavirus pandemic - see photo.

Box Tunnel

Box Tunnel: The engineer was Isambard Kingdom Brunel and it was constructed between 1836-1841 to a length of 3,212 yards. The western portal in Box was cleaned and restored in 1986 by British Rail, assisted by the Railway Heritage Trust, Wiltshire Council, Box Parish Council and private subscriptions to commemorate its 150th anniversary. Of the twelve or thirteen ventilation and light shaft holes ranging from 306 - 70ft, only five remain. Over one hundred men were killed in different parts of the works and in different ways - and many more were injured, some for life. For two days each year, the sun can be seen shining through Box Tunnel. Thirty million bricks were used, and 414,000 cubic yards of earth and rocks were extracted. The daily workers' wages were, Bricklayers 6s 0d, Miners 5s 6p, and Labourers 3s 6p.

Front garden of Box Village collector and antique steam enthusiast George Purser and his wife Pat.

Box Valley

Box Hill: The view from here across Box Valley at the very top of Box Hill as you enter Corsham on the A4 Bath to London road is stunning whatever time of year it is. It was not until 1756 that this stretch of road was established (now the A4). Previous to this, the turnpike route from Corsham to Box and Bath was via Chapel Plaister and over Kingsdown. In 1908 the old white crushed stone roads turned to black when the spraying of tar on roads commenced, with this London to Bath A4 road being amongst the first to be treated. In 1936 the London to Bath road was classified as a trunk road, thereby losing its old historic name, (*The Great Bath Road*) now known simply as the A4. The 1909 postcard image below was taken from the same spot as the modern photo above, with the main road unseen just to the left of the two cows.

Chapel Plaister

Chapel Plaister: The Pilgrims' Chapel at Chapel Plaister in the sketch below, originally published in 'The Gentleman's Magazine', of 1835 still looks much as it does [above] today. The Chapel is open each year on Wednesdays 14:00-16:00 between May and September and is full of history and artefacts. It is a fascinating place and well worth a visit. Tradition credits the building of the Plaister wayside Hostel and the sanctuary later known as Chapel Plaister c1235 to the 9th Earl of Warwick, Knight Crusader and Baron bu Plessis of Poitou. It stands beside what in previous times, was the pilgrims' route to Glastonbury. It was rebuilt in 1340 by Richard Plaisted of Castle Combe and again in 1450. In the mid-1700s when it was an Inn, it was one of the highwayman John Boulter's (also known as Poulter or Tom Baxter) favoured look-out haunts.

Claremont

Claremont: In 1807, Mrs Ellis purchased Claremont and converted it into a young ladies Boarding School at 14 Guineas per annum and 1 guinea entrance. In 1830 Ann Hemming was in charge and the girls were referred to locally as the *'Claremont Bulldogs'*. In 1866 Miss Lanham and Miss Turner ran the Claremont House school. In 1880 the Principal was Emma Butler. In 1891, Misses Agnes Tennant and Laura Rigden were the joint Principals. The Reverend Cecil Huntley Berry and Principle Mrs Berry purchased and managed the school between 1914 and 1920 (see photo below). During WWII it was occupied and used as a school for evacuee children. In 1945 it was purchased by the Rev. Percy Warrington and converted into a *'Home for Aged People'*. Photo above is courtesy of Warrington Care Homes the current owners.

Claremont girls doing physical excercises

Clinic: Corsham Clinic (below) once stood where the Porch Surgery is today (see photo above). St John Ambulance (including 1st aid training courses) used the old clinic for a while; along with Mr Starkey and Humphries the school dentists, plus….vaccinations, blood donors, chiropodist, hearing and eye tests, physiotherapy, baby weighing and even verruca removal! Until moving into the new building above in 1991 'The Porch Surgery' was based in a listed building on the High Street that had been *the doctor's house* as far back as anyone can remember. In the late 1940's early 1950's four doctors worked from the High Street surgery along with three part-time receptionists. Today, The Porch has five GP partners and employ a team of over thirty-five staff to provide medical services to Corsham and to the wider community.

Corsham Park - The Close: The fabulous image below, on the Corsham chemist Francis Baines' postcard of the early 1900s, was taken looking in towards Corsham Park at the end of the *Drung* (which is an old English word for passageway) opposite the end of Post Office Lane, halfway along Corsham High Street. The alleyway was also known as Lovers' Walk! The path leads into Corsham Park's South Avenue and onwards into Corsham Park. The Drung was used as a cricket field by the children of Henry Spackman. Henry first came to Corsham in 1838 to join his uncle and took over the High Street grocery business from him in 1868. His son Herbert went on to take many photos of Corsham. The Spackman children were obsessed with cricket and music and were involved with every local aspect both religious and secular.

The Close, Corsham.

Clutterbucks

Clutterbucks: The Clutterbuck family originally came from Flemish Clothiers who left Flanders during the persecution. Just left inside Corsham's St. Bartholomew's churchyard by the front gate is the grave of Lieutenant Daniel Hugh Clutterbuck (1828-1906) and his wife Sophia Ellen. In 1854 he was wounded in the right foot by a shell fragment in the Charge of the Light Brigade on 25 October. Daniel retired from the Army in 1855 and became a Justice of the Peace for Wiltshire and was Chairman of the Corsham Petty Sessions Bench. From 1903 he lived at Middlewick House in Pickwick where he died on 5 August 1906. Daniel's third daughter Katherine Mary Clutterbuck 1860–1946 became a nun known as Sister Kate and was a central figure at Australia's Parkerville Children's Home and *'mother'* to over 800 girls and boys.

Fragmented headstone epitaph - photo courtesy of Norman Duckworth.

High Street Corn Stores: This Grade II Listed building alongside the Town Hall at 67 High Street dates from the 17th &18th centuries and was originally, in part, a large malthouse (to the rear). In the 1950s the W.H. Wilkins' Corsham Corn Stores was a busy shop here - it even sold 'Lassie' a popular canned dog food at 1s 8p for an extra large tin, or 11p for the handy size. The building had been gutted in the mid-1980s and until very recently first housed the *'Dolphin'* chip shop and then *'Delicious House '* a ChineseTake-Away. The building was completely renovated in 2019 by JME Conservation who exposed as much of the internal fabric of the building as possible to allow the volume of the building to be enjoyed. It is now a new home for Stonewood Design, an architectural practice, based at West Yatton Lane, Castle Combe, Wiltshire.

Corsham Court

Corsham Court: The east side sketch of Corsham Court below, is by C.V. Fielding 1823 and titled *'Corsham House, Wiltshire: The Seat of Paul Methuen Esqr. M.P. for Wiltshire'*. There has been a house here since 978 when it was a summer palace for the Kings of Wessex. The property was part of the dowry of the Queens of England until Elizabeth I granted a leasehold. Thomas Smythe erected an Elizabethan Manor House on the site in 1582. In 1745 Paul Methuen purchased the house and it has remained in the Methuen family ever since. This privately owned historic house holds a significant art collection and along with the gardens, is open to visitors. It is also used by the Bath Spa University as a post graduate centre. The current owner is James Methuen-Campbell, the eighth generation of the Methuen family to live here in Corsham Court.

Cricket Ground

Cricket Ground: In the early Middle Ages sheep were penned here overnight inside the Pound (previously known as 'Wimblesteed') on their way from Salisbury Plain to the Port of Bristol. In the Station Road wall alongside the Bowls Club, you can still see the outline of the original Pound's gateway.

Corsham Cricket Club 1ˢᵗ XI 1889. Back Row left to right - L. Spackman, C.J. Mayo, A.C. Kinneir, J. Smith, W.G. Allard. Middle row - H.E. Mayo, Herbert Spackman, W. Spackman, W.H. Robinson. Front - C.F. Spackman and S.P. Kinneir. The 1889 team had one of its most successful seasons for many years and it's not surprising. Sep Kinnear and later, Jessie Smith's nephew Jim Smith both went on to play for England. Herbert Spackman is responsible for many of the old iconic photographic images of Corsham.

Cricket Pavilion

Cricket Club: Page 3 of the Wiltshire Independent, Thursday 2 May 1845: *"A Cricket Club was about to be formed in Corsham, under the superintendence and patronage of Paul Methuen, 1st Baron Methuen (1779-1849"*. The first newspaper report *(played against opposition)* was recorded as taking place against Bradford-on-Avon on Friday 28 August 1845 in a field belonging to Mr James Usher (Innkeeper at Corsham's Pack Horse Inn at the time). The original pavilion at Pound Pill was no more than a tent. A new wooden, thatched roof pavilion was built in 1878 and lasted until 1908 when it was replaced by a corrugated iron construction. This was replaced by a single-storey stone built pavilion erected in 1971 (see photo below). A 2nd storey was added above and the new building was opened in 1999 by David Gower.

Crook, Draper and Milliner

Crook Wholesale: G. D. Crook, Wholesale and Retail Drapery, Millinery, Outfitting, and Boot Establishment, occupied the two large Grade II houses just inside the High Street/Pickwick Road junction. These two houses (No.3 and No.5 High Street) were once known as 'North Wilts House' and 'London House' and in 1893 they belonged to Mr George Douglas Crook of the drapery trade. George joined the two houses together so that his premises presented a most attractive frontage of four spacious show windows, altogether about sixty feet wide. In 1914 No.3 High St. became *H.R. James and Son, the hardware shop following *Horace's marriage to Nettie King who was managing her father's shop there. In 1923 they moved into the larger premises alongside at No.5. No. 3 later became the clothes outfitters *Macmillan.*

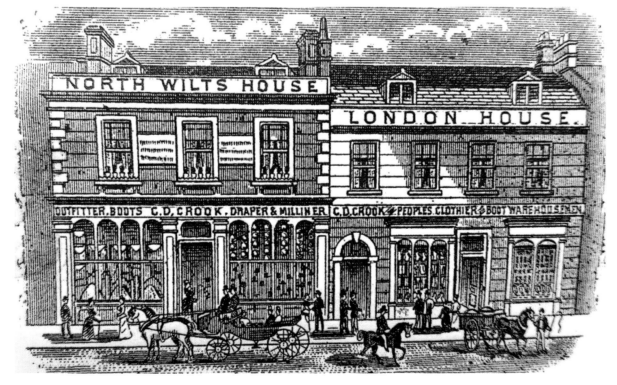

Cross Keys: The crossed keys symbolise the gold and silver keys of St Peter and represent the power of loosing and binding *(Matthew 16:19).* Above is a 1992 sketch of the 16th century Cross Key Inn by local artist Vic Woolford. The photo postcard image below was taken c1920. The building was purchased in 2020 and is now a private residence sympathetically restored by the current owners to retain its *olde world charm*. In the late 1800s the Inn was often used for inquests. The crossroads here has seen many deaths including at 7:45p.m. on the 21 November 1927 when a Mr Goulding sadly died after being hit by a car driven at about 40 miles an hour. In 2019 the crossroad junction was once again reconstructed to include new traffic lights, a new road layout to prevent overtaking, wider pavements and a pedestrian crossing.

Dry Arch

Dry Arch: This is an ornamental arch made of *'petrified'* stone built in Corsham Park to allow the Methuen family and their guests to walk uninterrupted beneath the public right of way. The public footpath passes over the dry arch in the middle of Mynte wood. It links Capability Brown's park with the land to the north, later landscaped by Humphrey Repton. Petrified stone, is the result of a tree or tree-like plants having completely transitioned into stone by the process of permineralization (in short, it's stone made out of trees). The arch is carved with the names and regiments of many a WW1 and WW2 soldier. The Dry Arch is an original feature of Corsham Court's two-mile 'Great Walk' now called the 'North Walk' (originally designed by Lancelot Brown in the late 1700's), which meanders through the planted 'Mynte' woodland.

APRIL: Private W. L. 24/4/17 of the 27th Battallion Canadians

Duke of Cumberland

Duke of Cumberland: The late 17th century Duke Of Cumberland Inn was situated at 15 Priory Street. It closed in 2008/2009 and is now Cumberland House, a private dwelling (and is a Grade II listed building). In the 1800s it was used to hold Corsham inquests. In 1870 the landlord was William Thomas then George Griffin. In 1889 the licensee transferred from John Batley to George Purnell. In 1891 Mrs Eliza Say was proprietor. In the latter years Arthur Bailey and his wife Marion (nee Say) ran the pub. It was renowned then for selling Scrumpy Cider and for its shove halfpenny board! The original bench (inset) opposite was a gift from Mr A E Pinnell. He was granted permission from Lord Methuen in 1954, on behalf of residents in Priory Street, to place a teak garden seat there for public use. Today's bench is not quite so grand.

Fish and Chip Shops

Fish and Chip Shops: Corsham has rarely been without a main fish and chip shop for well over 100 years. The first was Little's fish and chip shop at the end of a short alleyway exactly where the Newlands Road/Pickwick Road roundabout is. On the Married Quarters Site (MQ1) was Edgell's the very popular fish and chip shop, located behind the Community Centre opposite the Fire Station and at the bottom of Beechfield Road *(photo below)*. Edgell's shop was the mainstay during Corsham's 40s/50s/60s prefab bungalow era. Then came 'Turners' managed by Chris Turner and his wife Vickie's chip shop in the town centre feeding the hungry for many years along with Gerald Smith's Dolphin fish and chip shop to the right of the Town Hall. Today Tongs *(above)* is a favourite *'chippy'* on the corner opposite the Methuen Arms.

Football Club: Above is Corsham Town Football Club in Season 2020/2021 taken by © John Cuthbertson. Below, the oldest photo of Corsham Football Club was taken in the 1905-1906 season, showing Corsham Town Football Club Reserves - Champions of the Chippenham & District League. The first newspaper report appeared on page 7 of Wiltshire Times and Trowbridge Advertiser - Saturday 9 February 1878 *'Corsham v Melksham played on the Corsham ground on Saturday 2 February 1878'*. In 1893 Corsham became affiliated to the Football Association. The team was often referred to as 'The Quarrymen'. Corsham played on an area of land above the present-day Recreation Ground from 1912. After failing to move to a preferred new ground at the rear of 'The Grove', in 1949 they moved to the Southbank, in Lacock Road.

In 1973 a recently renovated and re-equipped building at the ground was completely destroyed by fire. In 1994 a replacement clubhouse was built. In 2001 floodlights were installed, a 112 spectator stand erected and hard standing built around the pitch perimeter. In the 2006/07 season Corsham Town won the Western League Premier Division and added a third successive Wiltshire Senior Cup victory, once again beating their local rivals Melksham Town. Justin Flowers was promoted to first team manager for the 2018/19 season. Due to the Coronavirus pandemic, the 2019/20 season was cancelled and all results declared null and void by the Football Association on 26th March 2020. In 2020 Club Photographer John Cuthbertson completed his 'Southbank Chronicles' - three comprehensive books on the club's history.

1954 Corsham Town FC and Chippenham Town FC Combined Charity Match: © Charlie Ralph

Garden of Remembrance

Garden of Remembrance

Garden of Remembrance: The memorial was opened by the Duke of Edinburgh on his first appearance at a public function on 1 November 1946 on land bequeathed by Miss Agnes Tennant and Miss L. Rigden *(the Claremont Ladies' School Principals 1891-1931)*. William David Lewis is one of 57 Corsham men who perished in WWII whose names are carved into the stone memorial here. He was a POW on the Japanese Ballalae Island as part of a work party of 517 British prisoners of war captured after the Battle of Singapore. They were tasked to construct an airfield after which the prisoners, including their commander Lt. Col. John Bassett, were all executed. The mass graves were discovered after the war. His granddaughter Gina Rae went there to see her grandfather's name on the memorial and in the early 1980s obtained his medals.

Golden Path

2015

Golden Path: The path started at the north end of Alexander Terrace opposite where the launderette is today and came out at the top of Post Office Lane. It was in 1898, when Corsham Parish Council agreed to build a path here lined with a 5ft high corrugated iron fence which began falling down as early as 1904, not helped by children finding sticks and rattling them noisily all the way along the fence despite a notice placed at the end of the path, *'warning persons against committing nuisances'*. The land originally belonged to Mr Richard Blanch who lived at 11 High Street, and it was called the 'Golden Path' to celebrate his golden anniversary at the time. **Photo bottom left:** The house on the far left centre was rented by Hezekiah Hancock in 1923, and then later by his son Bill who were both Coal Merchants in the yard here. The old *smelly* Corsham's Public loos were opposite. **Photo bottom right:** The large building in the centre was part of a second-hand furniture warehouse site owned by Mr Baker in Alexander Terrace who made good strong Windsor chairs for 5 shillings. The original wooden British Legion building can be seen on the right. In 1951, plans were submitted, to build a replacement cinema here for the Regal Cinema Co. Part of the original pathway still runs alongside the Telephone Exchange and the modern British Legion building.

Post Office Lane

← Corsham High Street →

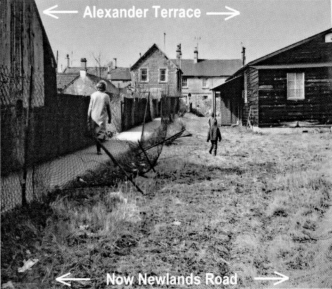

← Alexander Terrace →

← Now Newlands Road →

The Great Western Inn: On 1 December 1838 a man named Norris (a navvy employed in excavating the nearby railway cutting) was found dead here in the hay loft in what was then known as Mr. Salter's Rail Road Inn at the bottom of Pound Pill. It was later named 'The Great Western' after the railway that runs nearby through Box Tunnel. It was renamed as *The Royal Arthur* for a while. In 1907 the road that runs from here [21 Pound Pill] to Corsham Station (then called Stokes' Lane) was widened at a cost of £200. In 2018 this building was completely refurbished and extended, costing £290K. It reopened for business on Friday 2nd November in 2018 including a new restaurant overlooking the Ladbrook stream at the bottom of the garden. The new licensees are Michael and Kimara Yeomans who relocated from South Africa.

The Grove: This Grade II listed *Palladian style* house was built by Robert Neale in 1737 and extended in the early 19th century, and was once a Dower House *(i.e. available for use by widows of the Methuen family)*. The house, the wall, piers and gates and stable block and outbuildings are all Grade II buildings. An advocate of the Church of England's Temperance Society Rev. George Newham took up residency here in 1877. Although he preached abstinence he was married three times and sired thirteen offspring! His grave occupies a south corner of St Bartholomew's church. In WWII the stables were used as a First Aid post and housed the St John's Ambulance. In 1948 Corsham Football Club failed to move their ground from the Recreation Field into the field behind *The Grove* and they ended up in Southbank along the Lacock Road.

Grove House from the back.

CORSHAM. The Grove

1907

Guyers House

Guyers House: Originally built as a small farmhouse in about 1670 by a Mr Snelling, who named it Snellings. In 1678 it was sold to Edward Bayley who transformed it into a very substantial building. A map of 1773 shows that John Bennett owned the property renamed Guyers. John died in 1802 and by 1813 Thomas Pycroft owned the house. The 1816 Corsham Tithe Map shows Henry Hall Joy as owning this plot of land named 'Great Guyers'. In 1831 Reverend Timothy Conyers moved in with his mother. Between 1850-1858 Captain William Wallace Rooke lived there. Also previously once home to the Durnstervilles, Dickensons and to Colonel Handsford who added a ballroom in 1920. It was purchased in 1989 by Guy Hungerford and is now a 37 en-suite bedroom Hotel & Restaurant set inside 6 acres of beautiful gardens.

Early 1900s

1901 map

Hanning-Speke, John (1827-1884): Corsham has links to many famous people of note, but here is one whose adventures surpassed most. It was muted at the time that Speke's tragic death when aged 37, when he accidentally shot himself whilst climbing over a dry-stone wall when visiting his Uncle Mr J. Fuller at Neston Park on 15 September 1884 could have been a mishap or suicide! A memorial marks the spot on the edge of a field near the Horse and Jockey/Cross Roads Farm traffic lights on the B3109 road to Bradford-on-Avon. Speke was associated with discovering the source of the Nile in 1862 and the discovery of Lake Victoria as part of Burton's expedition to Africa in 1858. Burton had remained behind, ill in camp when Speke (once the best of friends with Burton) made the discovery, causing animosity between them.

Hare and Hounds

Hare & Hounds Inn: Eleazer Pickwick (1748-1837) ran a coaching business in Bath. His grandfather Moses Pickwick was a foundling abandoned in Pickwick, Corsham and given his names by those who found him there in 1694; named *Moses* after the Old Testament prophet and *Pickwick* (where he was abandoned). Moses lived in the Hare and Hounds Inn and worked there as an ostler. It is believed that Charles Dickens (1812 -1870) borrowed the name of *The Pickwick Papers [first published by Chapman & Hall in monthly instalments from March of 1836 until November 1837]* from the Pickwick surname emblazoned on the side of Eleazer's coaches when journeying along the London to Bath turnpike road. In 1984 the Bath to London Mail coach journey was re-enacted on 1 August stopping at the Hare & Hounds for a change of horses.

Hartham House

Hartham House: Originally a former 15th century Tudor farmstead owned by the Goddard family, it was replaced by Hartham House (now a Grade II listed building). Designed by James Wyatt, it was built 1790-1795 for Lady Anne James (nee Goddard). Since owned by several families; e.g. American exile Michael Joy and later his son Henry Hall Joy, Duckett, Goddard, Sir Benjamin Hobhouse, Methuen, Nicholson, Dickson-Poynder. At the turn of the century, Churchill and Asquith are known to have stayed in the house, as did H.R.H Prince Arthur and the Duke of Connaught and Strathearn. The gardens were landscaped by Harold Peto, of Iford Manor fame. Hartham Park was acquired by Jeffrey Thomas, in 1997 and is now an active business campus comprising of fully serviced offices, flexible work-spaces, and meeting and event rooms.

c1905

High Street Garage: Mr William Fry's late 1800s gift shop was on the corner here. He was an 'anti-vaccinator' and once had his goods seized as a passive resistor. In 1919 this building was sold by Mr Eli Merritt who had run a livery business with stables at the rear, to Harry Bowerbank the driver for Field Marshal Lord Methuen, then Governor at Malta. When Queen Victoria died, Harry was one of the four Marines guarding the body overnight. In 1938, Harry formed the Corsham Section of the St. John Ambulance Brigade. Harry caught pneumonia in 1954 after a hernia operation and the garage was subsequently sold to Mr H.W. Malpas. After the Malpas's, Jim Espin ran the garage from 1961-1971. The garage had a ghost of a small child in a nightgown; the patter of small feet was often heard there.

High Street Narrow Section

High Street Narrow Section: In 1839 the firm Beszant and Balch traded here as a butcher and abattoir (where the Corsham Book Shop is today). They had a slaughterhouse around the back (roughly where Boots the Chemist is today). It was common to see animal blood running down the High Street here. William Beszant passed away on 25th February 1967. In 1902, the Rev. Edward Gell's new wife Gertrude objected to the sound of the suffering from the poor animals in the slaughter house. Opposite (early 1900s) was F.G. Brett Jeweller and Watchmaker with his slogan, *'High Class Repairs. Choice Presents. Best and Cheapest'.* Before this section of High Street was pedestrianised and opened in 1976 (by TV celebrities Arthur Askey and Dickie Henderson), buses and lorries often became stuck in this narrow thoroughfare.

High Street Narrow Section

Narrow High Street: On the left in the photo above was once Tommy Ives' butcher's shop, then Derek Love - and now the Mother and Wild restaurant. The flower boxes here in the narrowest part of the High Street were introduced in August 2020. They were positioned to allow space for the queuing restaurant customers to be segregated *(so called social distancing)* from passing shoppers during the worldwide coronavirus pandemic. The yellow objects are an art installation in 2020 by Bristol artist Duncan Mckellar, who was commissioned to make these fantastic dancing sculptures using yellow foam scaffolding tubes. It was not only mothers with their prams who found it difficult to navigate what was once a very narrow two way street here, with even narrower pavements. Buses and lorries often became stuck here for hours blocking what was once a busy thoroughfare, prior to this section of the High Street being pedestrianised in 1973 when the new shopping precinct was built. In the 1800s a chain was stretched across this narrow street to corral cattle and sheep on their way to Beszant and Balch the butcher's abattoir/slaughter house premises behind where Corsham Book Shop is today. If you look on the pillars of the modern shops there today, you'll see cattle carved into the stonework in memory of the butcher's business. You can see their shop just to the left of the white door in the bottom right photo; those two buildings were demolished to make way for a new entrance into the modern *Martingate* shopping precinct from the High Street.

No. 40A High Stret: This building was part of the 120 years long Spackman and Sons family's Grocery and Drapery premises in the 1800s that spanned No's. 42 & 44 High Street. In March 1941 Alfred Charles Johnson a High Street grocer and confectioner was in trouble here with his hire-purchase payments and received a court order to pay back the £19. 17s. 6p. arrears otherwise his grocery van used for home deliveries would be recovered. In the 1950s the shop was named *B. Johnson Grocer and Confectioner*; they sold broken biscuits there too! It was later used as an office for Hancock's coal yard which was opposite and at the other end of Post Office Lane. The alleyway alongside here was called the 'Drung', also known as the Shrubbery, Janet's Close and Lover's Walk. Today, the *'unique hair'* shop occupies this building.

High Street South Entrance: The photo below is one of Corsham's famous old views which feature on postcards of the early 1900s. The group of boys are standing outside G.D. Crooks' the drapers shop which spanned no's 115 and 116 High Street until the early 1920s. William Charles King, an ironmonger, occupied the shop with the gaslight in the early 1900s; he also had a shop in Chippenham. This later became the No. 7 High Street *'Farthings'* Gordon Fraser Gallery (now David Ingram Estate Agents). Opposite was Cawte & Sons Plumbers and Decorators, which later became a cycle shop and garage for motor cars. On the left was G.D. Crook, Wholesale and Retail Drapery, Millinery, Outfitting and Boot Establishment who took over both (once known as) No.115 and 116 High Street buildings - now No's 3 and 3A High Street, Corsham.

Ice House: In 1816 the Hartham estate was purchased from the Goddard family trust by American exile Michael Joy who added an ice house (see photo below), at Hartham Park. This ice house subsequently served as an air raid shelter during the Second World War. The Corsham Park ice house *(above)* is in the middle of the park. An ice house is a structure built partly underground, for the preservation of ice for use during warmer weather. For centuries, ice houses were the only way that people could preserve and store their food. During the winter, ice and snow would be cut from Corsham lake or delivered by the 'Ice Man' in a horse and cart. The Corsham Park Ice House once stood alongside the 'Stew' ponds which were filled in, in 1798 before the eleven acre east Corsham Lake as we know it in its present location today was built.

2016

Ladbrook Cemetery: The Ladbrook Lane (then known as Squitters Lane) Cemetery was consecrated on 14 October 1911 by the Lord Bishop of Bristol (see photo below). It is a peaceful and attractive resting place to serve the residents of Corsham. There are 22 Commonwealth War Graves in Ladbrook Lane Cemetery. Eleven of which are First World War and eleven Second World War. These can be identified by the white gravestones renewed at the head of each grave. The small Chapel (now a storeroom) could accommodate 13 mourners and was designed by Corsham's William Osborne. He died of spotted fever, a form of polio, during WWI and became one of the first to be buried here. In 2020 a 2.2 acre extension to the graveyard was completed on the west side. It is anticipated that this is efficient for well over the next 100 years!

© John Cuthbertson

Ladbrook Cemetery 14 October 1911

Lady Methuen's Infant School

Lady Methuen's School: This 3-roomed school for poor children was funded by Paul Cobb Methuen in 1816. Sadly, he died on the 15th September 1816 and probably never saw the finished school. The Corsham County Junior School on Pound Pill *(now the Pound Arts Centre building south of the cricket field)* was later formed from the Lady Methuen's School for Girls (founded 1816), the National School for Girls (c.1840s) and the Corsham British School for Boys (c.1840). These schools came under the aegis of the Corsham School Board in 1893 and were finally merged there in c1923 The infants remained housed in the Methuen School which became the Corsham County Infants' School. Colin Hudd's c1926 photo below, shows Infant Class 2. Colin's father, Wilfred Reginald Hudd is in the front row, second from the right.

Lake: Corsham Lake was completed on 7 May 1798. From the late 1800s to the 1960s it was regularly used in the winter time for skating. The English author Sir Pelham Grenville (PG) Woodhouse (1881-1975) spent school holidays with a clergyman uncle nearby and was often taken to Corsham to skate on the lake in winter. In 1916 on Sunday afternoon 17 December, there was a beautiful sheet of ice on Corsham Lake. This attracted a large number of skaters and sliders and games of hockey and football were enjoyed! Herbert Spackman's photo of the skaters below included the humorous superimposing of the bus on the ice. In 1999 the lake was completely dredged and the surrounding pasture restored with 90,000 tonnes of silt being removed from its basin. The lake is now a haven for wildlife including hordes of Canada Geese.

Lightning Tree.

Lightning Tree: The 1907 postcard below, of a *lightning tree* in Corsham Park, is similar to the 2007 photo above, taken there in the early morning mist 100 years later. In July of 1907, five yearlings at Mr Uncles' Foscott Farm in nearby Grittleton were killed by lightning, an old couple were found unconscious in their cottage in Chippenham and the nearby Wesleyan Chapel was also struck. In the late 1700s Repton and Brown populated Corsham Park with many trees, including the screen of trees planted around the park to define its parameters and obscure the roads and fields beyond. During the late 1970s, thousands of Elm trees were felled across the Corsham Estate as Dutch Elm disease took hold. The *lightning tree* was more likely to be an old shallow rooted Oak not particularly well suited to the Park's shallow calcareous soil.

Corsham Park.

Mansion House

Mansion House: The Neale family are synonymous with this Grade II building built in Pickwick Road c1721-1723 and altered in 1897 by H. Brakspear. The sizes of the Neale family tombs at the rear of St Bartholomew's graveyard are testament to their wealth in better times. If you look on the pillars of the old main Mansion House entrance door you will see the c1700s scratch marks of the Neale children in the stonework showing their heights (see inset). Originaly formally known as Corsham House, where Corsham School (otherwise known as, 'The Classical and Commercial School') once existed with Charles H. Hulls, as its Principal. In the 1960/1970s it was a Youth Club. The modern square entrance building attached to the left of the Mansion House was completed in 2019 when it was transformed into a digital innovation and business hub.

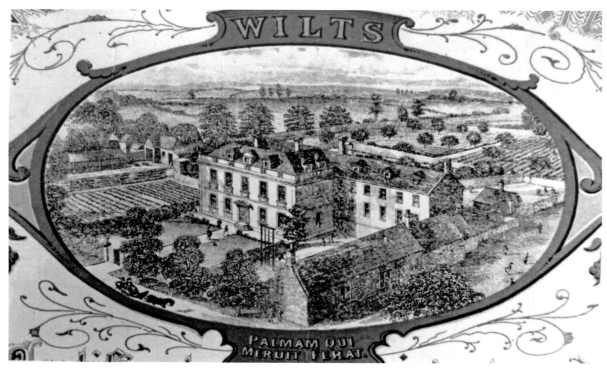

Market Place

Market Place: In 1285, a weekly market was granted, to be held here in the square on Fridays. In the image below, a Market Cross stood near the entrance of Church Street and in 1776 it was irreparably damaged by vandals (John Evans and brewer John Dalmer) who were fined £30 (£1,500 in today's money). On the left you can see the town pillory where miscreants were secured for the purpose of having rotten vegetables thrown at them! Men suffered their punishment here and any Corsham landlord watering down his beer would have had a *stint* here. The Town Hall, a one storey building, was erected there later with open arches in 1783 by Paul Methuen (see photo above) and known then as the Market Hall. In 1882 it was partly rebuilt by adding on a second floor and filling in the arches. It was renamed as the Town Hall.

Marsh and Sons

Marsh & Son: In 1914 Marsh & Son moved from 55b High Street (see Theodora's Flower Shop) into 21 Pickwick Road (see photo below). They sold up in the 1960's to George Smith who carried on running it under the name of Marshes until it went into receivership. Greta Harris (Wendy Kent's mother) ran it for the Receivers and continued trading there for three years until it was finally closed c1965. In more recent years one of the last banks in Corsham (the Nat West Bank) occupied 21 Pickwick Road before closing on 25 July 2014. For a short while in 2016 it was then transformed into an Italian restaurant named La Piccola Italia. In 2018 Immigration Enforcement officers raided La Piccola and found three illegal immigrants from Albania working there. It became 'Il Gusto' in 2018, then 'Prime Cut' in 2019 and is now' Restaurant 21'.

Martingate Centre: It is difficult to imagine that Mr Hulbert's stonemason's yard shown below in 1920, is where the Martingate Centre and its car park are today. The house rooftop in the background are in Post Office Lane. A small alleyway alongside the newsagent's shop (once Pickwick Papers) and the 1790 Congregational Chapel (now the Grounded Café) gave access to the yard from Pickwick Road. Originally called the Corsham Precinct when it was built in 1973, the Martingate Centre *(which includes the Newlands Road car park)* is home to over twenty shops in Corsham offering everyday supermarket essentials as well as individual items from local retailers and charity shops. The Martingate Centre Limited, a family ownership commenced in 2004 and was originally owned by Bill Hall; now carried on by his son Martin.

Maternity Hospital

Maternity Hospital: The photo above shows a reunion that took place here in September 2014, of nearly 100 people aged between 60-90 who were born there. In the mid-1800s Alexander House was home to Corsham's Dr. Alexander. In 1919 Miss Doris P. Chappell (of Hatts House in Box), who came from a family of music publishers and piano makers, converted the building (see photo below) into a Maternity Home (also known as the Corsham Nursing Home). It functioned entirely on a voluntary basis for over thirty years until 1951 when it was sold by Charles W. Oatley at the end of March and was no longer a Maternity Hospital. In 1954 the High Street's Alexander House was converted into Council housing flats. In 1955 plans were put in place to build 20 new flats behind for '*old people*' (later named as 'Holton House') in Post Office Lane.

Mayo Memorial

Mayo Memorial: Charles Thomas Mayo was one of the town's most famous residents; he lived in Corsham's Ivy House from 1868 to 1895. He became the first Vice-Chairman of the Corsham Parish Council and a Lawyer. He oversaw the construction of the pipeline which first brought fresh water to Corsham from springs above Lacock, six miles away. After his death in October 1895 aged 61, a memorial in recognition of his life and works was built at the end of Priory Street (once the corner of his garden), where it stands to this day. If you look up at the top front left corner of the memorial, you will see a small lead mouse, the *'signature'* of 'Lead Workers' David and Jess Bevan who restored the memorial in 2007. The memorial originally cost £115 10s in 1897 to build and in 2007 the restoration cost was *a little more* at £25,000!

Methuen Arms

The Methuen Arms: The Methuen Arms Hotel was built on the remains of a 14th century nunnery. In Tudor times this was the site of an impressive house, known as Winters Court, and in 1463 it was owned by the 'Nott family', one of whom was a Bailiff of Corsham. It became a public house in 1608 known as the Red Lion Inn. In 1799 the ownership passed into the Methuen family and the building was *renamed 'The Methuen Arms'*. In Victorian times, it was a Coaching Inn with stabling for 40 horses. John Sweatman, the landlord of the Methuen Arms in 1830, later committed suicide in Corsham Park in 1844 by poisoning himself. The Duke of Edinburgh played skittles at the 'Methuen Arms', when he was an Instructor at the Royal Arthur Petty Officer Training School in Westwells when he was 'courting' Princess Elizabeth in 1947.

Methuen Arms - Traffic Conductor

Traffic Conductor - Stephen (Stivvy) Hill: In the early 1900s he was known as the "Traffic Conductor", always to be seen opposite the Methuen Arms in Pickwick Road, with his crutches opposite the south end of Corsham High Street. He kept a box there to sit on, in front of the Grove House wall, directing the horse-drawn traffic. He lived in Paul Street and had a crippled leg. He passed away before WWII and before the introduction of much faster vehicles! You can see Stephen leaning against the wall with a few other gentlemen in the c1905 postcard photo below. In September 1923 he was knocked down and badly bruised, and it was thought that his ribs were broken, but happily Dr. G. Wood told him that was not the case. Above is the same view in 2020 looking exactly the same as it did 100 plus years ago.

Lord Methuen and family on the steps of Corsham Court

The Methuen Family: Here is Field-Marshal Paul Sanford Lord Methuen 3rd Baron Methuen, GCB, GCMG, GCVO Legion d'Honneur (1845-1932) on the steps and by Corsham Court's gates. A list of the Barons Methuen of Corsham Court follow: Paul Methuen, 1st Baron Methuen (1779–1849): Frederick Henry Paul Methuen, 2nd Baron Methuen (1818–1891): Paul Sanford Methuen, 3rd Baron Methuen (1845–1932): Paul Ayshford Methuen, 4th Baron Methuen (1886–1974): Anthony Paul Methuen, 5th Baron Methuen (1891–1975): (Anthony) John Methuen, 6th Baron Methuen (1925–1994): Robert Alexander Holt Methuen, 7th Baron Methuen (1931–2014): James Paul Archibald Methuen-Campbell, 8th Baron Methuen (born 1952). The heir presumptive is the present holder's half-brother, Thomas Rice Mansel Methuen-Campbell (1977).

In the centre are Field-Marshal Paul Sanford Lord Methuen and his second wife Mary Ethel.

Middlewick House

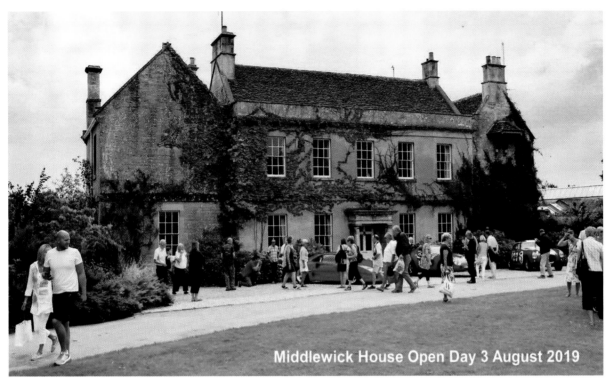

Middlewick House Open Day 3 August 2019

Middlewick House: This Grade II seven-bedroom listed Georgian-style building situated at the end of Middlewick Lane in Pickwick dates from the 18th century; the west wing is earlier. This was the home of Captain in the 8th Hussars Daniel Hugh Clutterbuck *(who was in the Charge of the Light Brigade in 1854)*; and he died here on 5 August 1906. Recently, it was purchased for an estimated £1 million by Pink Floyd drummer Nick Mason CBE and his wife Annette Lynton Mason (Nettie), who acquired it from the previous owners, Andrew and Camilla Parker Bowles *(Camilla, is now the Duchess of Cornwall),* in 1995. The garden contains a number of works by sculptor Simon Gudgeon. The gardens of Middlewick House were featured in the 2017 book The Secret Gardeners by Victoria Summerley and photographer Hugo Rittson Thomas.

1908

Monks Park Chapel

Monks Park Chapel: On the edge of Corsham, in Gastard sits the old quaint Monks Chapel. It was built in 1662 with stone taken from an open quarry in an adjoining field. It was built in response to the 1662 *Five Mile Act* passed by Parliament, when King Charles II and his Parliament took it upon themselves to revise the English Prayer Book. This lead to the Quakers secretly building Monks Chapel so that they could worship as their conscience dictated. The door under the Pulpit is reputed to lead to a secret underground tunnel through which the Minister could make his way to safety if the Chapel was raided by the authorities. The photo below was taken by Herbert Spackman in 1936 at the Chapel's 274th anniversary. In May 1986 it was officially accepted as a United Reformed Church and services still take place there each Sunday.

Monks Park House

1916

Monks Park House: *Grade II Listed building.* The name Monks originates from Henry Monke who was married to Agnes. Agnes later handed Monkes Park estate to her son William in 1406. John Hanning Speke who discovered the source of the Nile on August 3rd, 1858, died in a shooting accident whilst climbing over a wall in a field nearby whilst on a visit here to his brother Mr W. Speke J.P. of Monks Park. Lt. Daniel, Hugh (1828-1906) who was injured at the Charge of the Light Brigade lived here in 1889/90. Lady Alice Frances Holbrow Goldney resided here when she became Commandant of the Corsham Hospital at the Town Hall Red Cross hospital during the First World War. The female students at the Bath Art college in Corsham Court (1946-1986) had their hostel here. Monks Park house is now a private residence once again.

c1905

Monks Park Quarry

Monks Park Stone Quarry: The quarry here in Gastard on the outskirts of Corsham, started life in 1886 under the name of 'Sumsions' Monks or Monks North. In 1937 the UK MoD took it over for storage of ammunition and explosives. In 1941 the site closed and later reopened in 1954 for storage of Royal Navy equipment in the north part. Conversion was completed in 1956 with 250,000 tonnes of rubble being removed. In 1995 the site was sold to Leafield Engineering. In 2012 they redeveloped part of the site into a specially designed testing, re-calibration and prototyping centre and for the secure storage of UK MoD items. The 2020 photo above shows Leafield Engineering staff exiting in style from the Monks Park main entrance. In 2016 Hanson began quarrying stone there again, and later sold it to the Johnston Quarry Group. However, in March 2018 the quarry closed as the owners claimed it had become stagnant.

Bath Stoneyard at Monks Park on 29 October 1953, showing Bath Stone rangework and ashlar *(large square-cut stones, used as a facing on walls)*, and a vertical frame saw for cutting block into ashlar (sand is used as a cutting medium).

Newlands Road

Newlands Road: The 1816 Corsham Tithe Map shows Ezekiel Hanham as owning the plot of land called 'Newlands' in Corsham; *'New Land'* which Henry III gave to his brother Richard Earl of Cornwall; Newlands Road occupies part of this New Land! From the left in the old photo is the corner of Cawtes Garage, the rubble is the remains of the 1960's paint shop owned by Bernard Shillaker. In front was a fruit shop owned by Robert Fry. Behind is Mr W.H. Sealy the undertaker advertising a '24 Hour Service'. At the far end is Little's Fish and Chip Shop. The (now demolished) house on the corner was inhabited by Mrs Martin who used to sit outside with her dark green visor glasses in front of her window of religious artefacts. The Newlands Road town centre bypass with its new Pickwick Road roundabout was built here in 1962/63.

1963 by Richard Morling

Neston Post Office

Neston Post Office: Ran by Jack Swain in 1908. In 1946/47 the shop and Post Office was used by Prince Philip when he was based in nearby HMS Royal Arthur as an instructor. The c1930 photo below shows the Shell Mex petrol pump at the front and the Elley Green houses on the left horizon. The Post Office closed in 1961 when owners Arthur and Marjorie Cousins retired. The front room housed the shop and Post Office, while the couple lived in the rest of the house. Their daughter, Barbara Vaughan, donated the original Post Office counter to the Bath Postal Museum. Ray Watts remembers that the Shell pump was hand operated by Arthur. It had a glass container at the top that measured a gallon. Arthur would push a lever back and forth until the glass container was full, it would then empty the petrol into your vehicle through a pipe.

Pack Horse (now the Flemish Weaver)

Pack Horse: The 1905 photo below, shows R.D. McCarter's *Bath Electric Tramways* bus and its (32 maximum) passengers in 1905, in front of the Pack Horse which was once the Church House in 1794 (now the Flemish Weaver) alongside Corsham's Town Hall. The bus ran on Saturdays and Sundays only and took an hour to travel to Bath and 25 minutes to Chippenham. In the 1920s they ran char-a-banc day trips from Corsham to the Wye Valley. In the 1800s inquests were regularly held at the Pack Horse Inn. In 1844, James Usher was the landlord here; the Usher family later brewed beer on the Station Hotel site and later moved to Trowbridge to establish the well known Usher's brewery. The sign depicts a horse transporting wool for the weavers of Corsham. Drovers often stayed in the Inn whilst their animals rested nearby in the Laggar.

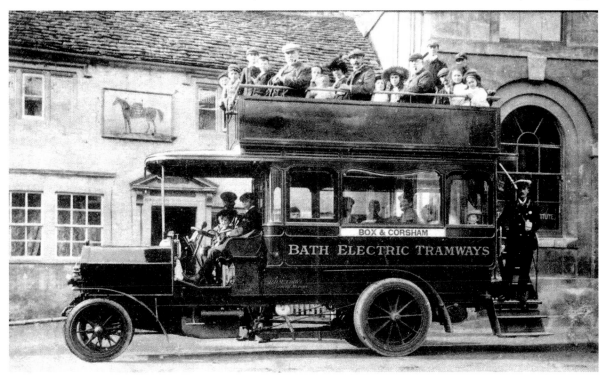

Parades: The photo above was taken looking down Church Street at the Remembrance Day Parade in November 2015. The photo below was taken on *VE Day 11 November 1946* looking back along Church Street. A Corsham V-Day 'Service and Parade' celebration was held in June 1945. It commenced with a parade of nearly 400 contingents from the Forces and Civilian organisations headed by the Regimental band of the Royal Army Ordnance Corps (R.A.O.C.), who marched down the High Street to St. Bartholomew's. Albert Sylvester (who lived in Corsham in his last years) *Principal* Private Secretary in the Government to Lloyd George typed the WWI Armistice Terms on his own Underwood typewriter and was personally entrusted by the Government to carry those documents to France in his leather briefcase.

Park 1912

Corsham Park 1912: A storm crossed the UK on the 26th of December with a fierce hurricane wind from the southwest lightning, heavy thunder, and rain. It caused the highest tide known for the past 40 years. Several trees came down and men from the Corsham Estate can be seen on the postcard below tidying up after the event. On the rear is written *'Corsham Court 1912 Jim and Bob'.* During the late 1970s, thousands of Elm trees (including those in the South Avenue originally planted in the 1700s) were felled across the Corsham Estate as Dutch Elm disease took hold. The South Avenue was replanted with Lime trees and is now a beautiful place to walk. The photo above shows Corsham Park in its full autumn splendour today. The Corsham Estate including Corsham Park has been owned by the Methuen family since 1745.

Pickwick Road Armistice Day 1946

Pickwick Road Armistice Parade 1946: The Armistice Parade above, is passing over what is now the Newlands Road roundabout. The buildings from right to left in the 1946 photo above are: the corner of what was Honeychurch's the hardware shop [now the Hong Kong House takeaway], Jack Martin's old house where his frail widow Mrs Martin used to sit outside in all weathers, with her dark glasses and a green visor, in front of her window which displayed an open bible along with other religious artefacts [this house was knocked down in the 70's to make way for the Newlands Road roundabout], a fruit shop owned by Robert Fry (later completely gutted in a fire in 1954), Cawtes Garage, the Regal Cinema, Corsham Club, St Aldhelm's Church and W. Hancock Furniture Removals yard/shed [now S&K Autos garage since 1980].

Pickwick Road Shops: In the older photo below, William Pearce was the grocer here in the 1870's and his daughter Miss Jane Pearce in 1889. To the immediate right of PEARCE's shop was Bert Barnes the Grocer and Confectioner (where Pickwick Papers once stood - now Londis). Note the gas street lamp on the corner shop (Gardiner & Cleverly (milliner). In 1860 a Gas works was built in Pound Mead and they were taken over by Bath Gas Company in the early 1930s. Barber and tobacconist Mr Goddard occupied the second shop front up from the corner. The c1960s photo above was taken in the days before the Newlands Road relief road and pedestrianisation of the south part of the High Street took place. The main route for traffic then, was along Pickwick Road and through the narrow High Street to the right of the photographs above.

Police Station: The first Police Station was in a building on the left-hand side of Post Office Lane near the corner with the High Street. The second Police Station, known as the County Police Station, was located in the building at 62 Pickwick Road (see inset). In 1950 a new Police Sub-Divisional Headquarters in Kings Avenue started to be built at the top of Priory Street in Corsham (see photo above). The Priory Street site was sold in 2014 and the building was knocked down between the 1st - 3rd July 2015 with the Corsham Police team moving into the new Corsham Campus in Beechfield Road in June 2014. The two original Corsham Police Truncheons from the 1800s, are *courtesy of Kieran Aust*. The 'WR' initials on the top truncheon commemorate King William, 'The Sailor King' who (at 64) began his reign from 1830 until 1837.

Poor House

Poor House: To the right of the Royal Oak in the High Street and behind the façade of 'Chairman Antiques' (who opened in 2020) once stood the c1728-1836 Corsham Poor House. In 1832 a sum of £200 was *ordered to be borrowed* for helping Corsham paupers to emigrate; 16 men, 10 women, and 27 children were selected. They were conveyed to Bristol in two covered wagons and safely put onboard their ship. In 1835 the Corsham Poorhouse consisted of five dwellings and housed 35 people. The maximum that could be held there were 90, but the greatest ever held in Corsham's Poor House at one time was 45. In August of 1974 the Poor House buildings were seriously damaged by fire. The Corsham Civic Society battled in vain to stop Wiltshire District Council from pulling down the buildings, but demolition commenced on 27 January 1976. Since the fire, the frontage has accommodated several shops e.g., E.S. Electrical Contracting, butchers North West London Meat Co. Coates and Sons, and Royal Wilts. Inside, is one of the original building's fireplaces. Below is the gable front end and a drawing by Corsham architect Oswald Brakspear.

Poldark comes to Corsham 2014

Poldark comes to Corsham 2014: In May 2014 Corsham's High Street became 18th century Truro on television for the BBC 1 Poldark series, starring the actor Aidan Turner. The photo above was taken on the junction of Church Street and the High Street. The old photo below was taken c1964 and from the opposite view looking down towards the same junction. Cheviot House on the right was once adorned in the early 1900s with the sign 'Alf Butt, Breeches Maker' a master tailor and proprietor of *'The Gymnasium'* a large room where films were shown. Alf was also Captain of the Corsham Fire Brigade. In the 1930s the building later became Miss Bailey's Private Primary School. In the early 1950s it was Young's Glove Factory. To its left was Daymond's the Baker. Opposite was 'The North Wilts County Supply Store, later the Co-op.

Pound Pill and Prospect

William John Home Mylne of Belmont Prospect:

On the back of the old photo card below is written, *'W.J.H. Mylne. Jean Ellen Mylne and John Everard Home Mylne about 1895. Outside their house 'Belmont'* (in Prospect) *Corsham, Wilts.'* William John Home Mylne was born in 1859 and died in Great Amwell in Hertford. He was a Surveyor and also lived for a time in Weston-super-Mare. Their other child was Jean Mary Home Mylne.

In 1911 he was listed in the 1891 Census as a Retired Surveyor and would have been about 36 years old when this photo was taken. In 1891 he was living in Clevedon Rd (Sabina) in Weston-super-Mare. In 1895, he was still living in *Belmont* in Corsham with their servant Annie Brownett.

Prefab Bungalows: In the build-up to World War II the population of Corsham was 3,754, in 1941 it rose to nearly triple at 9,268, including 3,000 men who were brought in to build the underground Ammunition Depot at Tunnel Quarry. The Bristol Aeroplane Company (BAC) relocated all of their production below ground at Spring Quarry. Eight hostel sites with simple single-sex accommodation, one-storey structures (prefab buildings) were built. Plus five married quarter's sites with two/three/or four bed-roomed prefabs built in pairs to house families. These sites were later demolished and replaced with council houses in the 1950s and 1960s. There are very few prefab bungalows remaining such as those at Thornypits. Below c1960 are Giuliano, Claudio and Domenico Carosi in Wardle Road with the Hare & Hounds pub top left.

The Priory - Heywood House: The grassy path in the old c1900 postcard follows the trajectory of the 1960s built Newlands Road, connecting Pickwick Road to the Cross Keys junction of the A4. Today, this view is blocked by large modern detached houses. Heywood House (now Heywood Prep School) was built on the site of an old Parsonage and Manor House called The Priory, associated with Corsham's Rectory Manor. Foundations of earlier buildings are known to be on this site. In 1856 the property came into the hands of the Methuen family. In 1951 it became Mrs W M Kidd's boarding school for 60 children and later by Bryan Fisher and his wife Irene. In 1980 it was sold by the Methuen family to Hugh and Sylvia Sivil along with a resident ghost. Today the school is part of the Wishford Schools group. The Head is Rebecca Mitchell.

Priory Street Hall

*Sylvia Spackman's sketch of the attic
(Herbert Spackman's sister).*

Priory Street Hall: In September of 1911, Herbert Spackman purchased a large hall for £50 which used to stand in the back garden of No. 80 High Street (then the Liberal Club's billiard table hall). It was moved to the side of Rose Cottage in Priory Street (now Dill House which Herbert bought in 1906 for £450). The old hall is still there and was once used for concerts, WWI sewing parties, Corsham Town Band practices, an outpost for the Glove Factory in Paul Street, for the Red Cross, used for evening dance classes, as a chapel for the Catholic Church's Father Ryan, before they moved into their current church in Pickwick in 1945, as the 'Fur and Feather Club' full of rabbits and birds, as a draughtsman's office, and also for a while as the 'Priory Street School' run by Herbert's wife *Daisy until 1932. Dill House is now a private residence.

Top Row: Peggy Rees, Helen de- ?, Betty Crouch, Teacher [***Daisy Spackman**], Dorothy Bowerbank, Muriel Osborne, Queenie Coates: **Middle Row:** Marjorie Ody, Peggy Taylor, Sheila Newell, Lilian Fricker, Vera Taylor, Willie' Angel?: **Front Row:** Jim Coates, Ron Bidmead, ???, Jack Taylor, Leslie Vowles.

Railway Station: Corsham Station on the Great Western Railway main line from London to Bristol was opened in June 1841. Goods traffic ended here in June 1963 and passenger services were withdrawn in January 1965. The station had a signal box, a goods yard and shed, two platforms and a large Station Hotel (now new housing). The goods shed is the only remaining building. Bath Stone excavated under Corsham was transported downhill on a network of tramways to the Corsham Station from the working quarries at the Ridge, Hartham, Spring Quarry and Monks Park. Alongside the Tramways road, stood a number of stonemason's yards such as the Station Road Stone-yard. The recent growth of the town of Corsham has led to demand for the station to be rebuilt and the campaign to reopen it continues.

Recreation Ground

Recreation Ground: When Corsham Football Club formed in 1884 they first played on land above the top of the Recreation Ground in Meriton Avenue. In 1921, to celebrate peace after WWI, the Parish Council created what is now known as the Recreation Ground (previously the Meriton Avenue field). This has remained a children's play area and sports field to this day. In the 1920s it hosted *'Children's Annual Sports Days'*. In 1926 a bandstand was built near the middle top entrance. In the early years, horses and sheep were allowed to graze here from 8pm to 11am and all day Sundays! In 1944 an air raid shelter was built at the bottom; it was converted in March 1946 into a Public Convenience for children and eventually demolished in 1969. Today it has a large area of open grass with a football pitch and children's play area.

Roman Coffin: On 3 October 1942 a workman digging the foundations for a new building on the WWII Central Ammunition Depot (CAD)'s Hudswell Laboratory site (**[A]** now Potley Lakes), *'chipped'* off the corner of a large coffin lid 9'' below the surface with his pick-axe. Inside was **[B]** a skeleton of a young Roman female between 16-20 years of age. Pieces of Roman pottery were also found nearby. Before construction of the Katherine Park housing estate, a search in vain was made to re-discover the coffin. An investigation in 2018 by this book's author Julian Carosi, discovered the coffin languishing in the basement under Corsham Court's Octagon Room **[C]** & the skeleton stored in three boxes in London's Natural History Museum [Ref: NHMUK PA SK 3520]. The coffin was once exhibited for a short time at Corsham Court.

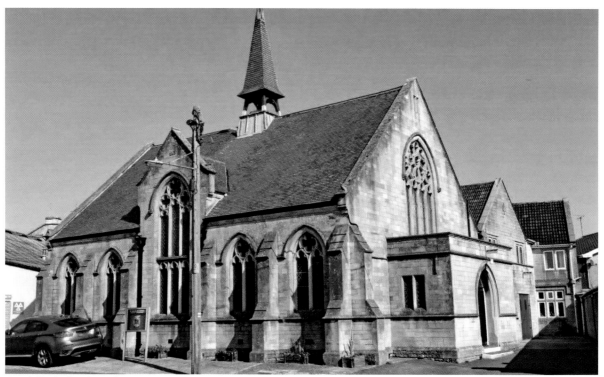

St Aldhelm's Church: Methodist United Reformed Church Pickwick Road: In 1790 a Congregational Chapel was founded (now the 'Grounded' Café) and continued in being until 1972 when the Congregational Church joined with the Presbyterian Church to form the United Reformed Church (URC). Approximately 150 yards away a Wesleyan Methodist Chapel opened its doors for worship in October 1878. In 1902, a larger church was built adjacent to the original one in Pickwick Road which then became the present church hall. From 1968 onwards, the two churches grew gradually together, sharing the worship occasionally and working together. Under the sensitive leadership of the ministers of that time, the two church families finally merged to become the Methodist United Reformed Church of St. Aldhelm's in 1984.

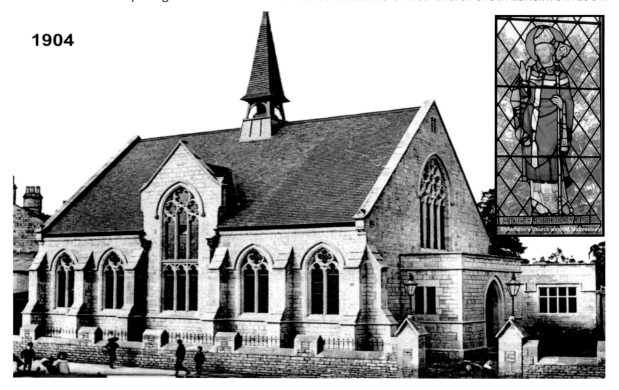

Saint Bartholomew's Church

St Bartholomew's Church: The town's church has been a centre of Christian worship for over one thousand years. The present church has 12th-century origins and underwent major Victorian restoration in 1875-8 by George Edmund Street, including rebuilding/repositioning of a new tower. The total cost of the work was £6,000 [£500,000 in today's money]. On the left outside wall of the church's porch facing west and looking back along Church Street, is a *gruesome* depiction of St Bartholomew the patron saint of the church holding his flayed skin. The vicar during 1902-1908, was Edward Gell (later Colonel Gell); he helped to select Westminster Abbey's Unknown Warrior in 1920. Inside the church to the left, is a list of the Corsham Vicars; the first listed in 1244 being *Ralph* and the present since 2015 is *Adam John Beaumont*.

E. Southy 1816

Saint Patrick's Church

Saint Patrick's Church: Now St Patrick's Catholic Church, the photos show the front and rear of what was the mid-Victorian 'Pickwick District School' built for up to 165 children in 1858 on land gifted in 1846 by Lord Methuen and his tenants, Sir Gabriel Goldney and Arthur Knapp. Teaching was conducted in a large room partitioned by a curtain. The school closed in 1922 and used as a glove factory during the 1930s. It later became a gas mask factory for a short while during WWII. The building was purchased in 1944 by Bishop Lee from the Diocese of Clifton, who blessed and opened it as the Corsham Catholic Church on 17 April 1945. It was dedicated to Saint Patrick as a tribute to the Irish workers and Father Ryan conducted the first Mass. The painting hanging inside by *A. Perrone* was presented by Italian prisoners in 1945.

Sarah Jarvis

Sarah Jarvis: St Bartholomew's churchyard contains a number of raised flat-topped 'table tombs', which were once very popular in this part of Wiltshire. An unusual inscription on a stone at the rear of the church commemorates one of Corsham's most famous *poor house* residents. The inscription reads, *'In memory of Sarah Jarvis, departed this life the 11th day of December, 1753, in the 107th year of her age. Some time before her death she had fresh* [a third set of] *teeth.'* It must be understood that she cut them, and did not obtain a false set from a dentist! The 1752 edition of the Worcester Journal reported that Sarah Jarvis, *'Grew a new set of toes, her former ones having rotted off about 16 years ago. Vast numbers of people from neighbouring villages daily resort to see her.'* Sarah Jarvis certainly managed to live to a ripe old age.

Sarah also liked apples, as page 9 of the Bristol Times and Mirror - Saturday 5 September 1885 reported the following: "Consult the old gravedigger respecting this phenomenon, and he will gladly tell the tale, "As ow the ould lady ad long kep er bed, an so wen opple time wur cum, she zed to er dater, 'I sh'd like sum opples to yeat,' and er dater, zed, 'Lor a massey, mothur! wat be taakin about, you can't yeat um, vor you got no teef;' and the ould lady zed 'rost um,' and zo th' ded, an she yeat um aal up. An so wen oppol time wur cum agen, she zed to er dater, 'I sh'd like sum oppols,' and er dater zed, 'Lor, mothur you can't yeat um, vor you got no teef;' an th' ould lady zed, breng em yer', an so th' ded, an th' nex day th' wur aal gon, and er dater zed, 'Wur be th' oppols gon to mothur?' an she zed, 'I yeat um aal;' an she zed, 'You couden, mothur, you got no teef;' and th' ould lady sed, 'Put yer vinger in me mouf, and see wur I hant; ' and zo sh' ded, and she ad vour, but sh' diden liv long ater."

Sarah Jarvis: Page 9: Bristol Times and Mirror - Saturday 05 September 1885

Corsham people evidently think otherwise. We will take an inscription from an old tombstone in this burying-place in evidence, although it must not be considered a fair sample : —

"In Memory of
Sarah Jarvis
who departed this Life the
11 Day of December 1753
in the Hundred and Seventh
Year of her age
Some time before her Death
She had Fresh Teeth.''

Consult the old gravedigger respecting this pheno-menon, and he will gladly tell the tale, "As ow the ould lady ad long kep er bed, an zo wen opple time wur cum, she zed to er datur, 'I sh'd like sum opples to yeat,' and er datur zed, 'Lor a massey, mothur! wat be taakin about, you can't yeat um, vor you got no teef ;' and the ould lady zed 'rost um,' and zo th' ded, an she yeat um aal up. An zo wen oppol time wur cum agen, she zed to er datur, 'I sh'd like sum oppols,' and er datur zed, 'Lor, mother, you can't yeat um, vor you got no teef ;' an th' ould lady zed, 'breng em yer,' an zo th' ded, an th' nex day th' wur aal gon, and er datur zed, 'Wur be th' oppols gon to,mothur ?' an she zed, 'I yeat um aal ;' an she zed, 'You couden,mothur, you got no teef ;' and th' ould lady zed, 'Put yer vinger in me mouf, and zee wur I hant ;' and zo sh' ded, and she ad vour, but sh' diden liv long ater.''

School Sports

Corsham School Sports: Originally this school building was the 1839 National British School for boys; it was later extended to accommodate 250 boys and 150 infants. In 1923 the girls' (from the Methuen School) and boys' schools were merged and the girls joined the boys on this British School site. It later became the Corsham County Primary School which moved across the road into new premises in 1994. The old school buildings were converted into the Pound Arts Centre which opened in 2007 after a £1.25m refurbishment. The following article appeared on **page 3 of the Western Daily Press - on Monday 18 July 1932.**

CORSHAM SCHOOL SPORTS: One of the chief events at Corsham School sports held in the Corsham Recreation Field was the competition for the Fuller Challenge Shield for boys.

This corresponding photo of the event appeared on page 27 of the Bath Chronicle and Weekly Gazette - Saturday 23 July 1932: This trophy had been held for the last three years by Ivy Lane School, Chippenham.

This year the result was: - 1 Corsham; 2. Ivy Lane; 3, Box. A girls' challenge shield contest resulted in Corsham being placed first and second, with Neston third.

The Hon. Mrs Anthony Methuen presented the prizes. Mr H. Burgess moved a vote of thanks to Mrs Methuen, and paid a tribute to Mr Dick Greenman and Mr H. B. Coates. On the call of Capt. H. H. W. Druitt three hearty cheers were given for the Hon. Mrs Methuen.

Scouts

Scouts: In 1997 Andrea Garrihy (1948-2016) who graduated from the Bath Academy of Art in Corsham in 1971 carved the Scout and Guide emblems for their Corsham headquarters. Field Marshal Lord Paul Sanford Methuen (veteran general of the Boer War) helped set up the scouts organisation with his friend Robert Baden-Powell. He also founded the Corsham Scout Group in 1908. Lord Methuen with two of his medals showing is in the 1917/1918 Corsham Scouts photo below. Today the Scout Group in Corsham provide adventurous activities for Beavers, Cubs, and Sea Scouts. The Scout Group in Corsham is run entirely by volunteers and they operate from a modern Scout Headquarters in 'The Laggar' and a boathouse, located in woodland adjacent to Corsham lake. Their website is here: *corshamscouts.org.uk/*

Smallpox House

Smallpox House: The Smallpox house in the centre of the photo below was originally a farm worker's cottage, part of farmer Burrow's Stowell Farm estate. The Corsham Vestry Minutes of 25 September 1893 record that: *'Isaac Sparks from Trowbridge be allowed 4/- as temporary relief having 2 children in the smallpox house, Cross Keys)'.* The last inhabitants of the Small Pox house at 5 Cross Keys, Corsham, were Mr Pat Sythes, his wife Isabel (also known as Jean) and their young son Michael. They moved across town to 14 Prospect (Stowford). The Smallpox House location is registered as plot 1304 on the Corsham Tythe Map and was demolished around 1966/67. In 2019 the Cross Keys crossroads were restructured to make it safer for traffic; the Cross Keys Inn (above centre) has since been sold and is now a private residence.

A.F. Smith & Sons: Previously originally part of Wakeley's of Corsham, a big clothing store in the 1890s, and Merritt's Cycles before becoming *A.F. Smith and Sons*. Builder Mr Frank Smith, his wife and their son Paul later emigrated to Australia. The store was bought by Vic Whiteley and Dolly Dunmore ran the shop with Derek Slater and his wife Margaret *(see inset)* along with Bengi the dog who loved sitting outside the shop. The building now houses 'PREVIOUS' a mini-department store selling vintage homewares and retro items, managed by owner, Nicola White, a former design history lecturer. The first Previous Homewares store in the High Street opened in 2015. They moved to their new, much larger premises across the road in July 2018. BBC presenter Paul Martin took over the old premises with his Table Gallery antiques shop.

South Avenue

South Avenue: Originally, three avenues of Elm trees radiated from Corsham Court to the North, South and East respectively. The South Avenue of trees stretching north/south from the gates of Corsham Court, across St Bartholomew's Church square and on to the War Memorial on Lacock Road was retained as part of the enhancements in 1749 by Paul Methuen who decided to improve his Corsham estate purchased in 1745. During the late 1970s, thousands of Elm trees (including those in the South Avenue) were felled across the Corsham Estate as Dutch Elm disease took hold. The avenue was replanted with Lime trees and is now a beautiful place to walk alongside Corsham Park. The avenue's early C18 gatepiers with moulded cornices and large ball finials are classified as a Grade II building. Corsham Park was once a deer park.

Published by Lewin Spackman. c1905

Springfield Community Campus: In 1943 the Beechfield Road Community Centre was built as a canteen and cinema serving the migrant community of munitions workers in WWII. The school photo above was taken outside the old Community Centre's main entrance in 1947. The Corsham Swimming Pool was added alongside the Community Centre in 1974. A newly completed 'Springfield Centre' with its sports hall was opened in 1988. The old Community Centre and purpose built Pickwick Road Library were demolished and replaced on 7 August 2014 when they became part of the centralised Springfield Community Campus run by Wiltshire Council. This created a modern focal point for Corsham leisure amenities including sports (e.g. swimming and indoor football), social clubs, meeting rooms, exhibition space and outdoor sports fields.

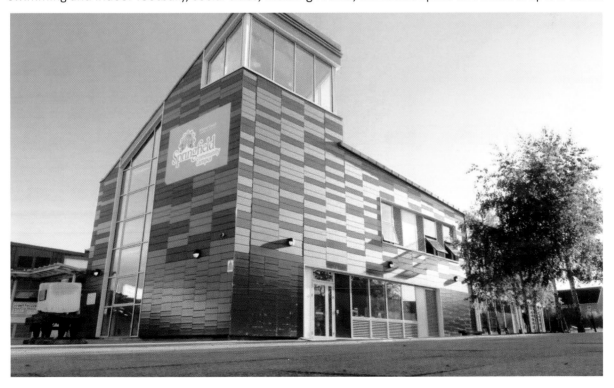

Springfield Community Campus: Above is the 1954 Corsham Centre Hockey Team courtesy of Gordon Williams and includes: Back row (left to right): Derek Love, George Dunning, R. Westwood, Kenneth Hayden, Cec Tanner, Ken Laney, Doug Hudd, R. Jackson. Front row, Philip Pope, S. Baker, Peter Snape, Anne Crowe, Barbara Clarke. This area of Corsham was once the Married Quarters Site No.1 of the three prefab bungalow sites built in Corsham to house workers. The old red-bricked Community Centre building shown below has been demolished and is now a car park for the new Springfield Campus building which can be seen looming up behind. In its day, the Corsham Community Centre was a popular social club with a busy bar area and large hall for pantomimes, drama and musical events such as disco nights and live music.

Starwell: The well is located underneath a line of pylons in a field just past Stowell Farm on the lane (1st left after the Cross Keys) from Corsham and Chippenham. To find the stars, filter the sediment through your fingers *as if panning for gold*. They are the tiny fossilised stem parts (columnals) of crinoids, millions of years old, a plant-like sea-creature commonly known as a sea lily and related to starfish. They are washed out of the underground bedrock over the millennia by the gentle action of the spring. The well was also a possible *stopping off* point on the pilgrimage route to Glastonbury which came westwards through Biddestone towards Corsham. There is no right of way or public footpath across this marshy field, so please ask the Stowell Farm owner's permission to enter his field before you make a visit.

Station Road Cottages

Station Road Cottages: The Joseph Goold photo of the Station Road Cottages below was taken c1875 in a time when there was a well in the corner of the garden here. Nine years after, these cottages were demolished and replaced by the house and garden that remains there today (out of picture) on the corner of South Street. The only two buildings along the Station Road hill at the time were the 1856 Gospel Chapel and the cottage opposite, now 19 Station Road. These can be seen at the top of the old photo below. The second wedding ceremony ever performed in the Gospel Hall, Corsham, took place there on Saturday 29 August 1936 between Cecil Archer a Corsham Court gardener and Miss Ena Louise Gillard youngest daughter of Mr & Mrs R. Gillard, Wellington, Somerset. Presents included one from Lord/Lady Methuen.

Tannery

The Tannery: In 1830, the Goold family from Farrington Gurney, Somerset established a Tannery (see inset) on land in the valley alongside the Ladbrook stream at the bottom of Pound Pill at the end of this lane in Corsham. They took residency in Ash Villa, Pound Pill along with 20 acres of land including a stone quarry. The private lane in the photos leads to where the tannery was once situated. It later became *'The Old Tan Yard Stone Works'* where Frank Davis had a stonemason's yard. Today, large pieces of discarded Bath Stone are occasionally discovered at the old Tannery site in Pound Pill. The site was purchased in 1986 by Brian and Sue Head, who set up home there with their herd of goats and three children, Christopher, Martin and Jeremy. Sadly, Brian Head passed away aged 76 on 5 November 2019. *R.I.P. Brian Head.*

Taxis

Corsham Taxis: Below are four of Jeffrey (Jobby) Johnson's "Corsham Taxis" (London cabs) at the top of the Recreation Ground in Arnolds Mead. The photo was taken c1982. The business, established in the 1970s was originally managed from a booking office opposite the Methuen Arms until c1980 (alongside Lady Methuen's School). The office then moved back home into 28 Arnolds Mead. The business was finally sold to Bill Hanley in 1986. Jeffrey's wife helped to run the business by taking calls and despatching the taxis. Jeffrey was very proud of his cabs and his wife Maureen always looked after the drivers, by making cups of tea and bacon sandwiches. On the wedding day of Prince Charles and Lady Diana, the cabs were adorned with Union Jack bunting. Maureen sadly passed away in November 2009 and Jeffrey in November 2016.

Theodora's Flower Shop: The Marsh family lived in nearby Chippenham's St Mary's Street in 1911. In 1913 they were established in the 'Marsh & Son Fish and Fruit Salesmen' shop (see photo below) in the 1906 building in Corsham High Street (now 55b High Street 'Theodora's Flowers, Plants and Home Decorations' shop - see photo above). In 1914 the Marsh & Son shop moved into larger premises around the corner at No. 21 Pickwick Road (see Marsh & Son for more). The building shown here, started off as part of the adjoining 'The North Wilts County Supply Stores'; later the *butcher's* part of the 'Cooperative Store'. If you look carefully above the '*Beehive 'Industry 1906'* stone carving on the adjoining No.55 (Garden Veterinary Group) building, the edges of the painted-over 'COOPERATIVE STORE' lettering can just about be seen.

Town Band

Town Band: The fabulous Corsham Town Band photo shown above was taken in the Arnold House garden in 1962 in front of the practice building. TOP ROW from left to right: Alan Horner, W. Philpott, Ben Havenhand, Tony Pike, Lewis Courilla, Jimmy Thorpe, Tony Forcey, Jack Heyward. MIDDLE ROW, Peter Boulter, John Springer, Colin Cox, Brion Bond, John Jenkins, John Rushton, Arthur Hulbert. Seated at the front, Ron Forcey, Pete Gale, Frank Fields, Evart Gough, Arthur Pike. The band were established in 1888 and are still going strong, *see https://www.corshamband.com/.* Below is the band in the National Brass Band Finals of Great Britain at Cheltenham Racecourse in 2017 - an achievement in itself. The coronavirus pandemic of 2020 stopped rehearsals and performances throughout the lockdown period in England.

Town Crier

The last Corsham Town Crier: Charlie Bethel born in 1881 was a young man who sought out opportunities when they arose and could turn his hand to just about anything. He became Corsham's last Town Crier. Charlie's 'claim to fame', was attempting to wheel a cubic foot of Bath Stone (1 ¼ cwt) 45 miles on a wheelbarrow from Corsham (via Bath, Saltford and Keynsham) to Bristol and back in twelve hours as a result of a wager! He finished five minutes *longer* than the stipulated time. Charlie may have lost his wager, but due to the *additional* collections and the *sympathetic contributions* received along the way, he boasted a total profit of £15 (£1,300 in today's money)!! Charlie can be seen in the photo below leading an Armistice parade through Corsham High Street in exactly the same spot as the modern photo above.

Town Hall

Town Hall: The Town Hall was originally built and known as the Market Hall in 1783 by Paul Methuen. In 1882 it was partly rebuilt by adding a second floor and by closing in the arches to become the Town Hall. Between 1914-1919 it became a WWII Voluntary Aid Detachments (V.A.D.) Hospital for the British sick and wounded. Lady Alice Goldney was the Commandant there until the Hospital closed in 1919. A total of 875 soldiers were treated there by 75 nurses - at an annual cost of £2,500. This was one of Corsham's proudest and greatest achievements. The Town Hall clock was erected in 1897 in commemoration of Queen Victoria's Diamond Jubilee. Stocks once stood at the left hand corner. Today, the Town Hall serves as the Corsham Town Council Offices and a public venue available for hire in the High Street, Corsham.

UFOs: Above is the entrance to what was RAF Rudloe Manor. The present Manor House was built in 1685 on an earlier construction. It was bought for £14,000 from the Danish Countess Raben by the Air Ministry in 1941. In the 1950s they began collecting reports of flying saucers, crop circles, and even abductions by aliens! They received many hoax reports which they had to investigate. It closed in 2000. All the UFO information was sent to the National Archives at Kew. Around 5% of the cases could not be explained. The project ran for over 50 years until 2009 when the MoD's UFO inquiry desk - Sec(AS)2 was closed down. Today the location is fenced off, monitored by cameras and guarded by dogs.

Royal Naval Stores Depot Copenacre - now housing.

Underground: In the year 670 Saint Aldhelm (645-709 A.D.) threw down his glove at Hazelbury Hill and *'Bade them Digge and they should find great treasure'* meaning the Box Freestone. During WWII the Bristol Aeroplane Company produced engines underground. And the 125 acre Tunnel Quarry, Corsham Armament Depot (CAD) at Hudswell contained 3000,000 tons of explosives and cost £4,500,000 to build (£143m in today's money). In 1956 construction on the underground 'Burlington' bunker to house the Government in a Cold War began. From 1945-1996 the Royal Naval Stores Depots were housed in three of the underground quarries. Today, the underground continues to be mined for Bath Stone by the Lovell Stone Group at Hartham Park Quarry and by the Blockstone Quarry group who operate in Park Lane Quarry.

Corsham Armament Depot (CAD) underground loading platform.

War Memorial: Built to remember Corsham's First World War (1914-1918) and later the Second World War (1939-1945) casualties. It was built at the end of the South Avenue, on land donated by Field Marshal Lord Methuen *(standing left of the monument).* There were 115 lives lost in WWI and 52 lost in WWII. A total of 36 war memorial designs were sent in before the final one by Mr Woolley of Frome was chosen. The memorial was built by Osborne and Sons stonemasons of Corsham. The War Memorial was unveiled by Lady Methuen on 28 January 1921 with the words, *"To the Glory of God, and in memory of our beloved soldiers".* The memorial is mounted on three steps of Atworth stone, the body is made of Box stone and the panels are made of Forest of Dean stone. A remembrance parade is held here each November.

Weavern

c1920/30s

Weavern: In the 1950/60s before Corsham Swimming Pool opened, Weavern in the Box Valley is where Corsham children learnt to swim in the Bybrook alongside Weavern Farm. In 1332 the farm was occupied by William De Vevere. The earliest mention of a mill being there, was in the *Wiltshire Historic Environment Records* of 1536 and named as *Weversmylle*. The mills were used for grinding grain or *fulling* (a woollen cloth making process which involves the cleansing of cloth - particularly wool to eliminate oils, dirt, and other impurities, and making it thicker). In 1793 it was used as a paper mill. The Poulsom family ran it as a farm for 30 years from 1881. In the early 1950s the last people to live at Weavern Farm were George and his wife Flossie Groves. Today the buildings are derelict and access to the brook is completely fenced off.

Early 1900s

Weavers Cottages

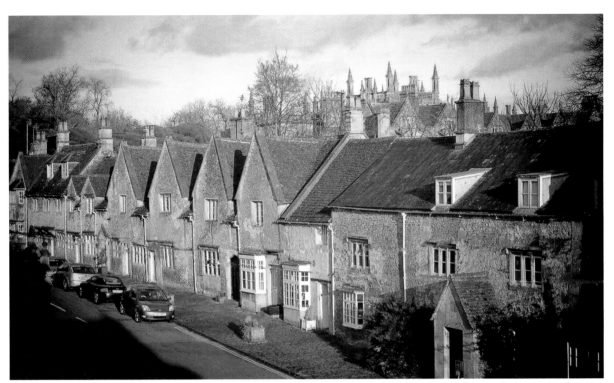

Weavers Cottages: Also known as the The Flemish buildings were built in the 17th century for the Huguenot weavers who fled their country because of religious persecution. The cottages were built by Paul Methuen (then Lord of the Manor) to house the weavers and to encourage them to stay in the area. The old black and white photo of the Weavers Cottages below was taken on 27 October 1953 and looks almost exactly the same as it does today! Corsham's first Fire Station c1800 was located in the Flemish buildings at 90a High Street (now the Curtain Workshop). The fire engine consisted of a small horse drawn cart, with leather buckets and 150 feet of leather hose! In 1897 they moved into a small building at the end of Priory Street and later c1908 into the building opposite Ivy House (now the Nursery at Heywood Prep School).

Women's Institute

Women's Institute: On Tuesday 3 June 1919 a meeting presided by Mrs Emily Georgina Jane Fuller of Neston Park. They agreed to form the first Corsham Women's Institute to be run on non-political and non-sectarian lines. Mrs Fuller was elected as President, Hon. Secretary Miss Tennent and Treasurer Miss Rigden. New members were enrolled at a second meeting on June 17th. On 7 December 1919 they organised a Variety Show at the Town Hall featuring the Bohemian Concert party from Bath. The WI photo below taken in 1956 advertises 'Teas, Sandwiches, soft drinks and Cakes'. In November 1940 they invited all the WWII evacuees in Corsham to their monthly meeting in the Town Hall; 130 to 140 people turned up! In 2019 a celebration was held in Springfield Community Campus to mark 100 years of the Corsham WI.

Sadly, the Corsham WI ceased on 21 January 2020

Acknowledgements.

I wrote this book *Corsham Revealed Now and Then*, so that I could share once again with you, my love of how Corsham became what it is today.

The detail has been gathered together from many sources. Firstly, once again, I'd like to say a very big thank you to my two proof readers, my partner **Susan Duparcq**, and to **Christine Coutts** who *dotted all the i's and crossed all the t's* for me; without them, the book could never have been finished!

And a big thank you to those sources and people mentioned below. Thank you once again to all those at the *Wiltshire and Swindon History Centre* in Chippenham for their advice and for helping me delve deep into their comprehensive book, record and newspaper archives.

And to **Chris Perry** and **David Kilmurray** at Corsham Print for a great job in printing this book.

Thank you to the **British Newspaper Archive** with their repository of old newspapers.

―――――――

Below is a list of the sources for which I am truly grateful. I have strived to be meticulous in my recording of source detail - and can only apologise if anyone has been missed out.

Note: This is a self-publishing and self financed book and not a profitable commercial enterprise.

The acknowledgment listing below is *roughly* in alphabetical order!

Thank you very much…………to all of you [from Julian Carosi].

NWELYAMAID?

Acknowledgements go to:
Aberdeen Press and Journal : The **Archive** Photographs Series - Corsham : Photographic View Album of Corsham by T. **Baines** : **british**listedbuildings.co.uk/ : Corsham Revealed Trilogy by Julian **Carosi** : http://**corshambusiness**show.co.uk/ : **corshamchamber**.com/ : Corsham **Civic Society** : John **Cuthbertson** : Christopher **Dallimore** : Stephen **Flavin** Corsham Born and Bred books : **Gazette** and Herald : Chris **Hall** : www.**higgypop**.com : Ernest and Margaret **Hird** : **history.wiltshire**.gov.uk/ : Joe **Jones** : Wendy **Kent** (nee Harris/Greta Harris) : (Eight Years of Cricket 1848-1928 by H.S. **Lakeman** : Lord Methuen and the British Army - Failure and Redemption in South Africa By Stephen M. **Miller** : Richard **Morling** : The **Ports** of the Bristol Channel 1893 : Charlie **Ralph** : James **Rowe** : 'A Corsham Boyhood', the Diary of Herbert **Spackma**n 1877-1891 : **swheritage**.org.uk : www.**warrington**residentialcare.org.uk/ : **Western Daily Press** : en.**wikipedia**.org : Wiltshire and Chippenham History Centre : **Wiltshire Times** : **Wiltshire Times and Trowbridge** Advertiser : **Witness 200** - A history of Independent Christian Witness in Corsham by David J. **Williams** : http://www.**wiltsunited**churches.org.uk/ : Corsham **Women's** Institute :: Corsham Facts & Folklore by Patricia **Whalley** : Becca **Wilkin :**

ISBN 978-1-5272-7770-0

The Author Giuliano (Julian) Carosi.

My name is Giuliano (Julian) Carosi; I was born in the Greenways Hospital Chippenham on 1 July 1952 and have lived in Corsham all my life. My father Francesco was an Italian prisoner of war who loved this country so much that he decided to stay here after WWII.

My father met and married my Italian mother Fiorenza (Enza) here in England and they set up their first home at 2 Wardle Road, in one of the old prefab bungalows just behind the Hare and Hounds. I have two brothers, Domenico Roberto, and Claudio Angelo and three lovely daughters, Melanie, Isabella Lucia and Sofia Francesca. And two lovely grandchildren George Dalibor and Ella Lucia.

I studied English at the Corsham School and later at Chippenham College. The old black library hut behind the Fire Station *(see Chapter 22 of my first book Corsham Revealed)* was a favourite haunt of mine as a young child. This is where I became enchanted with a love of the written word. The *Famous Five* books by Enid Blyton were one of my favourites in those days and this is where my sense of adventure was kindled. Now, it is Charles Dickens and all of the other Classic novels of the Victorian era.

For a number of years, I was Editor of the National Football Referees' Association magazine *'Refereeing'* and nowadays I run a local Facebook page called *'Mr Corsham'* where I encourage discussion on Corsham's history with the members. My first book in 2018 *Corsham Revealed* seems to have been a great success and spurred me on to write my second book *Corsham Revealed More,* my third book *Corsham Revealed Three* and now this, my fourth book *Corsham Revealed Now and Then.* I am retired after a long career as a civil servant working in several Government departments in and around and *deep underneath* Corsham.

I live near the cricket field in Corsham with my dear partner Susan Elizabeth in our lovely bungalow. My interest in the history of Corsham began after winning the, *'Know Your Corsham'* history competition in 1979. Since then, I have been gathering facts and stories for many years and discovering the many hidden places during my love of walking along the many public footpaths in and around Corsham. I feel as though I've covered just about every square inch of Corsham in my long years - above and below ground!

I once thought that Corsham was a sleepy little town with very little history of mention. How wrong I was. In this, my fourth book, my aim is to share even more of my findings with you. Once more, I hope that my fourth book changes the way you perceive our little town. It does for me!

If you would like to contact me, I would love to hear from you.

Email me at: *juliancarosi@corshamref.org.uk*
Regards,
Giuliano (Julian) Carosi
November 2020